GROUNDCOVER
SERIES

Text research: Richard Ashby

Acknowledgements

I am grateful for the assistance of countless people at the university colleges and institutions included in this book. Special thanks go to the staff at Cambridge Central Library and Peter Hill at The Eagle.

I would also like to thank Richard Ashby whose text research skills have, once again, proved invaluable, Angela Dixon, Dennis Nail, Caroline Plaice, Robert Reddaway, Margaret and Frank Turner, Peter, John and Jill Sells, Donald Greig, and finally, Antony Jarrold, Caroline Jarrold, Sarah Letts, Reina Ruis and all at Jarrold Publishing.

John Curtis

Front cover picture: King's College Chapel
Back cover picture: Punts on Mill Pool

Designed and produced by Jarrold Publishing, Whitefriars, Norwich NR3 1TR

All photographs © John Curtis except as follows: pages 100, 101, 102, 103, 104, 105, 106, 107, 124 © Queens' College, Cambridge.

Copyright © 2000 Jarrold Publishing

ISBN 0-7117-1126-7
Printed in China.

2/00

PUBLISHER'S NOTE
Variant and archaic spellings have been retained in quoted material, while the modern spellings of place names have been used in headings. The inclusion of a photograph in this book does not necessarily imply public access to the building illustrated.

Cambridge

JOHN CURTIS

JARROLD
PUBLISHING

King Henry VIII statue on Trinity College Great Gate. In place of the sceptre King Henry is holding a wooden chair leg, placed there many years ago as a student prank.

CAMBRIDGE

GROUNDCOVER
SERIES

Punts, Quayside

Contents

Introduction

Cambridge – the name evokes many unforgettable images: the grand architecture of the colleges, the pastoral calm of the tree-lined Backs, the bustle of bicycling students on King's Parade, and the serenity of the Christmas Festival of Nine Lessons and Carols from the magnificent King's College Chapel. These are just some of the unique facets of this historical university city.

When the first scholars arrived in 1209, Cambridge was already a flourishing market community that had grown from a Roman fort in the first century, a Saxon settlement during the Dark Ages and a Norman stronghold.

For centuries the relationship between the townsfolk and the scholars was not harmonious, and privileges conferred on the university often resulted in rioting and violence. Today, 'town and gown' happily co-exist amid the many contrasting features of Cambridge. To walk around the city is to discover a mix of medieval, Tudor, Georgian and Victorian architecture – the quaint winding streets and passages, the wide stately courts, the green and peaceful spaces beside the River Cam, the busy shops and market stalls of the town centre. It is, perhaps, hard to believe, as one takes in this ancient setting, that Cambridge is at the forefront of science and technology, and is often referred to as the 'Silicon Fen'.

While it is principally the fame of the university and its buildings that attracts visitors to Cambridge, it is the timeless charm of the city and its way of life, sitting beneath the vast fenland skies, that leaves the lasting impression.

Just as writers and artists have been and continue to be inspired by the sights and atmosphere of the town, so the modern photographer cannot fail to be almost overwhelmed by the creative possibilities that it presents.

I was already familiar with Cambridge when I began work for this book, but in the year that I spent taking the photographs presented here, I found myself again surprised and delighted by the characteristics of this fascinating and beautiful city.

JOHN CURTIS

left: Wren Library, Trinity College

ST JOHN'S COLLEGE
GATEHOUSE

The Gateway of *St John's*, with its
four tall turrets and battlements
between…will show to what glory
early sixteenth-century brickwork
can attain. This gateway [is] the
noblest in Cambridge…

E. A. R. ENNION
*Cambridgeshire, Huntingdonshire
and the Isle of Ely*
1951

ST JOHN'S COLLEGE
NEW COURT, CLOISTER

The Evangelist St John my patron was:

Three Gothic courts are his, and in the first

Was my abiding-place, a nook obscure;

Right underneath, the College kitchens made

A humming sound, less tuneable than bees,

But hardly less industrious…

WILLIAM WORDSWORTH
From *The Prelude: or Growth of a Poet's Mind*
1850

ST JOHN'S COLLEGE New Court *above,* Bridge of Sighs *right*

It is said that an undergraduate of St John's was once lounging on Trinity Bridge just before dinner, when the reverend and learned the Master was returning from his daily canter. He rode up to the youth with the remark, 'Sir, this is a place of transit and not of lounge.' No attention was paid to this, and the remark was repeated with yet more force. 'Sir, are you aware what the bridge of Trinity is made for?' 'Yes, sir, to see St John's new buildings from.'

William Everett *On the Cam: Lectures on the University of Cambridge in England* 1869

ALL SAINTS' PASSAGE

Cambridge is a delight of a place,
now there is nobody in it. I do
believe you would like it, if you
knew what it was without
inhabitants. It is they, I assure you,
that get it an ill name and spoil all.

THOMAS GRAY
Letter 12 August 1760

ALL SAINTS' GARDENS

This garden marks the site of the
Church of All Saints in the Jewry,
built in the fifteenth century and
demolished in 1865. The cross
commemorates some of its
distinguished parishioners.

TRINITY COLLEGE HALL *left,* AND GREAT GATE *above*

The dinner this day is rather better than usual, for it happens to be dedicated to one of the great saints in the English calendar, and on the saints' days poultry and ducks are immemorially added to the ordinary masses of beef and mutton… Everybody is in a tremendous heat and steam, particularly the waiters, who are on the look out that too much shall not be eaten.

WILLIAM EVERETT *On the Cam: Lectures on the University of Cambridge in England* 1869

TRINITY COLLEGE
WREN LIBRARY

The spacious Classes, which are thirty in Number, are of Oak, which Time has reduced to the Colour of Cedar: But the great Number of scarce and valuable Books and Manuscripts they contain much better deserve our Attention; and amongst other Curiosities in the Library, are an *Egyptian* Mummy and Ibis, given to the Society by the present Earl of *Sandwich*, on his Return from his Travels.

THOMAS SALMON
The Foreigners Companion Through the Universities of Cambridge and Oxford
1748

TRINITY COLLEGE Great Court

The first quadrangle is of immense extent, and the buildings that surround it, with their long, rich fronts of time-deepened gray, are the stateliest in the world. In the centre of the court are two or three acres of close-shaven lawn, in the midst of which rises a splendid Gothic fountain, where the serving-men fill up their buckets.

Henry James *Portraits of Places* 1883

TRINITY LANE

…there is a method of spending the intervening hours between breakfast and dinner, which is not wholly disagreeable. It consists of leaning out of the window, and expressing your opinion of every woman that passes, in audible terms…what delicate young lady – one of the reader's sisters, for example – would object to the expression, 'What a slap-up gal!' or, 'Isn't she a stunner?' interchanged amongst each other, at the tops of their voices, by a party of young fellows at the first-floor window.

JOHN SMITH
Sketches of Cantabs
1849

TRINITY LANE

Imagine the most irregular town that *can* be imagined, streets of the very crookedest kind, twisting about like those in a nightmare, and not unfrequently bringing you back to the same point you started from…

CHARLES ASTOR BRISTED
Five Years in an English University
1851

TRINITY HALL

I remember a friend who came to see Cambridge for the first time, and strolling into the garden after breakfast, found it so strongly impregnated with the genius loci that he decided to cut short his round of sight-seeing at its first stage. Sitting there all day, he felt that he had imbibed the very essence of Cambridge life.

LESLIE STEPHEN
Life of Henry Fawcett 1885

CLARE COLLEGE

Few College edifices convey such a sense of unity as these of Clare.

Edward Conybeare *Highways and Byways in Cambridge and Ely* 1923

CLARE COLLEGE
BRIDGE

A feature of the bridge is the incomplete ball. The story goes that Thomas Grumbold, the architect, was so unhappy with his fee that he determined that the bridge would never be finished – and it wasn't!

CLARE COLLEGE
GATES

Everyone is struck with the neatness, the perfect finish, and the high degree of positive beauty which belongs to Clare…It has, too, an ancient and very noble avenue of limes. The avenue is closed by a handsome iron gateway, which opens on a pleasant lawn, known as Clare Hall Piece…

FREDERICK ARNOLD
*Oxford and Cambridge
and their Colleges*
1873

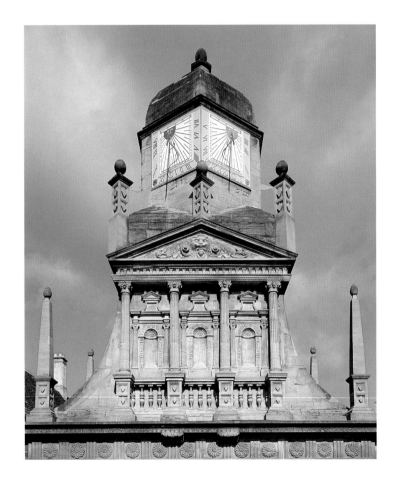

GONVILLE AND CAIUS COLLEGE
GATE OF HONOUR

…by reason of its very dottiness, the Gate of Honour is one of the memorable sights of Cambridge.

JOHN JULIUS NORWICH
The Architecture of Southern England
1985

GONVILLE AND CAIUS COLLEGE

There was a young student of Caius
Who dabbled in every disease;
But his girl – well, he shocked her,
This embryo doctor,
By dissecting the bodies of fleas.

The Granta 31 May 1889

The college was founded by Edmund Gonville in 1348 and re-established by John Kees (who Latinised his name to Caius) in 1557.

ROSE CRESCENT

This poem in bronze by C. S. Calverley (1831–1884) marks the site of Bacon's tobacco shop. Although a brilliant undergraduate, Calverley was expelled from Oxford for getting drunk, smoking, keeping dogs and scaling walls at night. Cambridge was more tolerant of his excesses and he excelled in its more liberal atmosphere, winning prizes, becoming a fellow and gaining admiration for his light verse. He died after a period of ill health following injuries sustained during a skating accident.

MARKET STREET *right*

A remarkable discovery made during building work was this perfectly preserved Art Nouveau shop front, a unique survival in Cambridge.

GREAT ST MARY'S CHURCH

At Cambridge, there is a great deal of church-going…The whole University is supposed to go at two o'clock to the sermon in Great St Mary's Church. It does not all go by any means. The reverend Master of Trinity has a weakness for ordering such of his own subjects as he meets, about the hour, to go.

WILLIAM EVERETT
On the Cam: Lectures on the University of Cambridge in England
1869

ST EDWARD'S PASSAGE

You are inclined to throw aside the books recommended by your tutor, and adopt a course of reading better suited to your taste. Beware of the first step to idleness and folly.

Hints to the Fresh-men at the University of Cambridge
1807

HAUNTED BOOKSHOP
St Edward's Passage

When a youth, possessing an ardent
thirst for knowledge and wisdom, is at
once entered into this seat of learning,
he finds himself surrounded by almost
all his heart can wish for – books,
tutors, lectures; and, what many a
neglected genius languishes for in
vain, retirement and leisure to
profit by his other advantages.

R. B. Harraden
History and Description of the
University of Cambridge
1822

CAMBRIDGE
FROM THE TOWER OF GREAT ST MARY'S CHURCH

Cambridge brings back a jumble of pipes and chimneys and pinnacles, leading up from security to adventure…nights when we merged with the shadows and could see the world with eyes that were not our own.

WHIPPLESNAITH
The Night Climbers of Cambridge
1953

OLD SCHOOLS
KING'S PARADE

The splendid Palladian façade facing Great St Mary's Church masks a complex of earlier buildings, including a medieval teaching building. Here students as young as fourteen years of age embarked on seven years of study – all instruction was in Latin and exams were oral.

PLEASE
NO DRINKS
FOOD
ICE CREAM

KING'S PARADE

The tradesmen in the better parts…keep first-rate and high-priced goods, especially the hosiers, tobacconists, and fancy dealers; while booksellers and stationers abound and flourish. The best shop windows are to be ~n, as a rule, in King's Parade, Trinity Street, and St Andrew's Street.

~SEPH CLARKE ISARD The Illustrated Guide to Cambridge and Neighbourhood by a Resident of Trinity c.1889

KING'S PARADE

If you have not been at Cambridge for some years, you are struck by…the cleanliness, cheerfulness and prosperity of the town, and by the pleasant, picturesque streets…

FREDERICK ARNOLD
Oxford and Cambridge and their Colleges
1873

OLD PUBLIC LIBRARY
Wheeler Street

Distinctive yellow-brick municipal buildings were opened in 1862 incorporating a new public library. A fine circular reading room, added in 1884, boasted marble columns and a distinctive domed roof. The library moved to Lion Yard in 1975 and the building was skilfully transformed into the Tourist Information Centre.

KING'S COLLEGE
CHAPEL, STONE SCREEN

This external screen is
the creation (1824–8)
of William Wilkins, not
for nothing the son of
a theatrical manager.

NORMAN SCARFE
Cambridgeshire – A Shell Guide
1983

KING'S COLLEGE
GATEHOUSE

The curfew tolls the hour of closing gates,

With jarring sound the porter turns the key,

Then in his dreary mansion slumbering waits,

And slowly, sternly quits it…

J. DUNCOMBE
From 'An Evening Contemplation in a College'
1823

The poem is a parody of
Thomas Gray's 'Elegy Written in a
Country Churchyard'.

KING'S COLLEGE Gibbs' Building

Now sheds the sinking Sun a deeper gleam,

Aid, lovely Sorceress! aid thy Poet's dream!

Samuel Taylor Coleridge
From 'Lines on an Autumnal Evening' 1793

KING'S COLLEGE Chapel

…every traveller on the rising ground for miles away, sees looming up before him, sparkling like silver in the sunlight, the majestic proportions of the fairest temple in England.

William Everett *On the Cam: Lectures on the University of Cambridge in England* 1869

THE EAGLE
BENE'T STREET

…the Eagle, once the Eagle and
Child, still discloses a courtyard
curiously galleried…

CHARLES G. HARPER
The Cambridge, Ely and King's Lynn Road:
The Great Fenland Highway
1902

THE EAGLE
AIR FORCE BAR

In the Second World War this pub
was a haunt of both US and British
Air Force crews stationed around
Cambridge, who wrote their names
and squadron numbers in candle
flame and lipstick on the ceiling of
one of the bars. It has become a place
of pilgrimage for their families and
friends, who come from all over the
world to see this extraordinary sight.

ST CATHARINE'S COLLEGE Gates

Above the main entrance gate is a golden Catherine Wheel, the symbol of the saint's martyrdom.

ST CATHARINE'S COLLEGE Main Court

…on our left…St Catharine's. King's follows. We used to be vulgar enough to say that though a cat might look at a king, Kings looked down on Cats.

SHANE LESLIE *The Cantab* 1926

50

CORPUS CHRISTI COLLEGE New Court

[Corpus Christi] possesses a ghost which is still heard occasionally. It is said to be the ghost of a young girl of seventeen who on her father's discovery of her in her undergraduate lover's rooms died of fright.

How to See Cambridge: a Really Useful and Interesting Guide to the Town and University 1928

CORPUS CHRISTI COLLEGE Old Court

No other court in Cambridge is so redolent of the Middle Ages.

John Julius Norwich *The Architecture of Southern England* 1985

PEMBROKE COLLEGE GARDEN

[The] Garden is large, well laid out, full of Fruit, and has a good Bowling-green in it. The North Wall of the Garden, which is very long, and reflects the warm Rays of the South Sun, makes the Walk which runs parallel to it the best Winter Walk in Town.

THOMAS SALMON
The Foreigners Companion Through the Universities of Cambridge and Oxford
1748

PEMBROKE COLLEGE Old Court

Henry VI always had a great affection for this college which he called his
'adopted daughter'. In a charter granting lands to the college he spoke of it as
'The eminent and most precious college, which is and ever hath been
resplendent among all places in the University'.

PEMBROKE STREET

I past beside the reverend walls
In which of old I wore the gown;
I roved at random thro' the town,
And saw the tumult of the halls;

ALFRED TENNYSON
From 'In Memoriam A. H. H.'
1850

PITT BUILDING
TRUMPINGTON STREET

The Pitt Building is named after Pitt the
Younger, who came up to Pembroke College
when he was fourteen years old. It was built
in the early nineteenth century to house the
University Press which had been established
in 1534. Cambridge was the first university
to have its own press.

CHURCH OF ST MARY THE LESS (LITTLE ST MARY'S) WASHINGTON MEMORIAL

Godfrey Washington was great-uncle to George Washington, first President of the United States of America. The coat of arms of the Washington family is believed to be the origin of the 'Stars and Stripes'.

Near this Place lyeth the Body of the Late Rev.ᵈ Mr GODFREY WASHINGTON of the *County of York. Minifter* of this Church and *Fellow* of Sᵗ Peter's Colledge Born July the 26ᵗʰ 1670. and Dyed the 28ᵗʰ day of Sepʳ 1729.

LITTLE ST MARY'S LANE

The town is govern'd by a mayor, and aldermen. The university by a chancellor, and vice-chancellor, &c…in some cases the vice-chancellor may concern himself in the town, as in searching houses for the scholars at improper hours, removing scandalous women, and the like.

DANIEL DEFOE
A Tour Through the Whole Island of Great Britain
1724–26

FITZWILLIAM MUSEUM
TRUMPINGTON STREET

…perhaps the finest classical
building which has been
erected of late years in this
country. Its exterior is very
imposing, and the breadth of
the street allows it to be well
seen. The architect was George
Basevi, unhappily killed by a
fall from the western tower
of Ely…

Handbook for Essex, Suffolk,
Norfolk and Cambridgeshire
1875

FITZWILLIAM MUSEUM
PORTICO CEILING

The wealth of the Fitzwilliam is so
great, one's eagerness to get inside
so pressing, that one seldom
bothers to look at it very carefully.
This is a pity; for though the
building falls some way short of
classical perfection, it has much to
interest and even instruct.

JOHN JULIUS NORWICH
The Architecture of Southern England
1985

PETERHOUSE

Thomas Gray had an irrational fear of fire. He had an iron framework erected outside his window in the College, to which he could attach a rope to escape the burning building. One night the alarm was given, the poet rushed to the window, slid down the rope and plunged into a bath of water which practical-joking students had placed at the bottom! As a result he moved across the street to Pembroke College.

PETERHOUSE
OLD COURT

It has nurtured men not only of distinction but of fame…

CHARLES G. HARPER
The Cambridge, Ely and King's Lynn Road; The Great Fenland Highway
1902

Peterhouse is the oldest college in Cambridge, founded in 1284.

FORMER ADDENBROOKE'S HOSPITAL
TRUMPINGTON STREET

…the front of the building presents a noble façade, great variety and picturesqueness being obtained by the judicious use of stone, terracotta and encaustic tiles, and coloured bricks…

The Lancet 28 April 1866

Addenbrooke's Hospital has been relocated outside the town; this building, renovated and enlarged, is now the Judge Institute of Management Studies.

HOBSON'S CONDUIT
TRUMPINGTON ROAD

A handsome stone conduit, of an hexagon figure…(the benefaction of the celebrated Hobson the carrier)…furnishes the middle of the town with water…

Hobson rendered himself famous too by furnishing the scholars with horses; and making it an unalterable rule, that every horse should have an equal share of rest and fatigue, would never let one out of his turn; from whence the proverbial saying,

Hobson's Choice: This or none.

A Concise and Accurate Description of the University, Town, and County of Cambridge 1785

The conduit was moved to its present position from Market Hill in 1856.

HOBSON'S BROOK Trumpington Road

Water from the Nine Wells, just outside the Cambridge boundary, is brought to the city in an artificial channel alongside the Trumpington Road. It runs down the gutters of Trumpington Street and feeds the ponds at Emmanuel and Christ's Colleges.

ST PETER'S TERRACE

The houses and business buildings are constructed mainly of local yellow brick, which is rather dead in effect by itself, but gives a good foil for green trees or other relief.

Joseph Clarke Isard *The Illustrated Guide to Cambridge and Neighbourhood by a Resident of Trinity c.1889*

TRUMPINGTON ROAD

From the great west door of this [Great St Mary's] church, the mile-stones in the neighbourhood take their measurement. Those on the London road, set up at the expense of Dr Monsey, of Trinity Hall, are generally affirmed to be the first of the kind in England.

R. B. HARRADEN
History and Description of the University of Cambridge
1822

DOWNING COLLEGE

In many ways, Downing, lying on the outskirts of Cambridge, makes the most pleasant impression of all the smaller colleges. An American would salute it as the only College possessing anything worthy to be called a 'campus'…it suggests an adapted country-house far more than an adapted monastery…

FRANCIS GRIBBLE
The Romance of the Cambridge College
1913

EMMANUEL COLLEGE
ARCADE, FRONT COURT

It was established by Sir Walter Mildmay in 1584. 'I have set an acorn,' he replied to Queen Elizabeth, who told him she had heard he had 'erected a Puritan foundation' – 'which when it becomes an oak, God alone knows what will be the fruit thereof.'

Handbook for Essex, Suffolk, Norfolk and Cambridgeshire 1875

EMMANUEL COLLEGE FRONT COURT

Emmanuel [College]…sent to New England, not Gentlemen Adventurers, but Pilgrim Fathers – far more than its just share of Pilgrim Fathers – no less than twenty-one of them. Above all, it sent them John Harvard, whose money endowed, and whose name is borne by, the greatest of the Universities of the New World.

FRANCIS GRIBBLE *The Romance of the Cambridge College* 1913

CHRIST'S COLLEGE GREAT GATE

Over the gateway the central coat-of-arms is
supported by two *Yales* – mythical beasts that
possessed the remarkable ability to rotate
their horns.

CHRIST'S COLLEGE MASTER'S LODGE

…to acknowledge publicly with all grateful Minde, that more
than ordinary favour and respect, which I found above any of
my Equals at the hands of those courteous and learned Men,
the fellows of that Colledge wherein I spent some Years…

JOHN MILTON *An Apology for Smectymnuus* 1641

CHRIST'S COLLEGE Fellows' Garden

Christ's College – the college of Milton and of the 'Platonists'…is chiefly interesting from its associations with the author of *Paradise Lost*. His rooms are still pointed out; and a mulberry-tree, said to have been planted by him, is still most carefully preserved in the garden.

Handbook for Essex, Suffolk, Norfolk and Cambridgeshire 1875

CHRIST'S COLLEGE Second Court

…at this time it is tolerably quiet…it is the quiet of luncheon. In less than an hour a few pianos will be heard jingling – the tutor here is not severe; only, whatever you do, don't play with the windows open during chapel.

JOHN BICKERDYKE *With the Best Intentions: a Tale of Undergraduate Life* 1884

CHRIST'S PIECES *left,* AND WITH ALL SAINTS' CHURCH *above*

Through Christ's Piece there surge, morning and evening, the inhabitants of much of east Cambridge to and from their daily avocations; and on Christ's Piece, when their work is done, elderly men play at bowls during the long evenings of spring and summer. On two nights in the week a band plays and hopeful youths clink little boxes for the support of the executants.

BRIAN W. DOWNS *Cambridge Past and Present* 1926

CHAMPION OF THE THAMES
KING STREET

…if [the rowing man] does get drunk, he does it with a will, probably by a rapid internal combination of champagne and milk punch.

LESLIE STEPHEN
Sketches from Cambridge, by a Don
1865

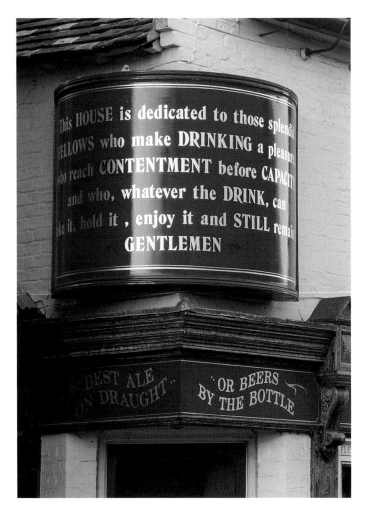

JESUS LOCK

Another day when with my friend by Parker's Piece I said, 'where by the bye is the river?' Neither of us knew, but having asked once or twice, soon made out our way to it…Afterwards, a walk by the waters of the Cam was my favourite way of spending the afternoons.

ALFRED HARRY LAWRENCE
Reminiscences of Cambridge Life by D. C.
1889

JESUS COLLEGE GATE-TOWER

You approach Jesus in much the same way as visitors used to find themselves approaching Mussolini – at the far end of a long, straight walk calculated to induce proper feeling of respect and awe.

JOHN JULIUS NORWICH *The Architecture of Southern England* 1985

JESUS COLLEGE CLOISTERS

…the very character of the colleges is monastic…the whole organisation being clearly borrowed from that of a convent, and recurring in their cloisters, gardens, butteries and kitchens…

WILLIAM EVERETT
On the Cam: Lectures on the University of Cambridge in England 1869

BOATHOUSES RIVER CAM

The season of greatest attraction for the outside world in this direction is the
latter part of the May Term – say the first fortnight of June – when the boat races
between the best eight-oar crews of the various colleges take place. Then for
several days half Cambridge seems to spend its evenings down the river.

JOSEPH CLARKE ISARD
The Illustrated Guide to Cambridge and Neighbourhood by a Resident of Trinity c.1889

FORT ST GEORGE IN ENGLAND MIDSUMMER COMMON

There has been a pub here since at least 1724. The building marks the site of a lock and sluice which maintained the level of the River Cam back through the town, and the publican had the responsibility of operating the lock. Originally called 'The Sluice', the pub was renamed in 1820 after a fort at Madras in India.

KETTLE'S YARD
ART GALLERY

[Kettle's Yard] was the home of Jim and Helen Ede who befriended and encouraged young aspiring artists and helped them financially by buying their pictures. In 1966 the Edes gave their home and collections to the University of Cambridge.

Cambridge Official Guide
1997

CASTLE MOUND Castle Street

…built in 1068 by William the Conqueror to hold Hereward the Saxon and his East
Anglian fellow-patriots in check…It never accumulated any legends of sieges or surprises,
and of military history it had none whatever…It is not the purpose of a castle to invite
attacks, but by its very menace to overawe and terrify…That Cambridge Castle not only
never fell, but was not even menaced, is the best proof of its power.

Charles G. Harper *The Cambridge, Ely and King's Lynn Road: The Great Fenland Highway* 1902

PORTUGAL PLACE

Portugal Place would make an ideal setting for a Jane Austen novel, with its Georgian town houses, its historic church and churchyard and its proximity to the town centre. There is little commerce, no motor traffic and an atmosphere of refined seclusion.

SARA PAYNE *Down Your Street: Cambridge Past and Present* 1983

MAGDALENE STREET

The houses are low and antique; sometimes their upper storeys project out into and over the narrow pathway, making it still narrower; and their lower storeys are usually occupied as shops – tailors and booksellers being the predominant varieties.

CHARLES ASTOR BRISTED *Five Years in an English University* 1851

MAGDALENE COLLEGE *above*, **AND COLLEGE CHAPEL** *right*

At the end of the eighteenth century and until about 1830, the Magdalene undergraduates, on account of their temperate habits, had a reputation for drinking tea, and they were accused of choking up the river with tea-leaves. Their first racing boat, launched in 1828, was called the *Teakettle*.

F. A. REEVE *Cambridge from the River* 1977

MAGDALENE COLLEGE

…the sight of its old walls, here dipping in the stream with a river walk, there resting on what is thought to be part of the outworks of the vanished castle.

ARTHUR MEE *The King's England – Cambridgeshire* 1937

MAGDALENE COLLEGE PEPYS LIBRARY

Samuel Pepys ('a very industrious and curious person' – John Evelyn) left his famous library to Magdalene College, stipulating that no new books were to be added and none thrown away. The collection of 3,000 volumes remains complete in the original bookcases, each book standing on its little wooden block to bring all the tops in line. His *Diary* is here too.

MAGDALENE COLLEGE
Main Gate

…I took my boy and two brothers, and walked to Magdalene College and there into the butterys, as a stranger, and there drank of their beer, which pleased me, as the best I ever drank…

Samuel Pepys *Diary 25 May 1668*

CHURCH of the HOLY SEPULCHRE
(Round Church) Bridge Street

Inside it retains its original form…But, in 1842, restorers set to on the remainder of the fabric with pious intent and unfortunate results.

E. A. R. Ennion
Cambridgeshire, Huntingdonshire and the Isle of Ely
1951

It is one of the four surviving twelfth-century round churches in England.

MAGDALENE BRIDGE *above,* MITRE TAVERN Bridge Street *right*

The vice-chancellor sometimes visits the taverns and other public-houses in person; but the proctors do it very frequently, and have power to punish offending scholars, and to fine the public-houses who entertain them after eight in the winter or nine in the summer.

Revd. C. Crutwell *A Tour Through the Whole Island of Great Britain; Divided into Journeys* 1801

THE BACKS
CLARE BRIDGE AND KING'S BRIDGE

…in all our tour of England has been nothing to equal the picture of Cambridge as we glide in a boat along the River Cam, or as we saunter at the Backs and stand on the bridges.

ARTHUR MEE *The King's England – Cambridgeshire* 1937

THE BACKS TOWARDS ST JOHN'S COLLEGE

…this Cambridge water architecture…[makes] the slow journey by punt along the College Backs, by the soft lawns and weeping willow trees, into the only architectural experience of the kind that can compare to being rowed in a gondola down the Grand Canal.

SACHEVERELL SITWELL *Sacheverell Sitwell's England* 1986

UNIVERSITY LIBRARY

For many months, since its steel skeleton appeared on our horizon, awkward pauses at our tea-tables have been covered with polite skirmishes on the subject of the Library tower, whether it is, or is not, A Mistake.

M. P. S. W. 'The Tower' *The Cambridge Review 6 June 1934*

THE BACKS

…the delightful walks at the back of the colleges…are laid out in avenues of limes, and elms, and horse-chestnuts, and the various Gothic buildings form a succession of delightful combinations with the masses of rich foliage.

The Eastern Counties Railway Illustrated Guide 1851

QUEENS' COLLEGE Mathematical Bridge

This famous bridge is a replica of the one erected in 1749, which was designed on mathematical principles by William Etheridge. The tradition that Isaac Newton was the designer is incorrect; he died more than 20 years before it was built.

QUEENS' COLLEGE RIVER CAM AND THE GROVE

The greatest beauty of this college is its grove and gardens; which, lying on both sides of the river, are connected with each other, and the college by two bridges of wood…the gardens being very extensive, well planted with fruit and adorned with rows of elms, and fine walks…

A Concise and Accurate Description of the University, Town, and
County of Cambridge 1785

QUEENS' COLLEGE Cloister

The cloister leads back to monkish times, and has a more monastic air, than even that of Jesus College, as being more narrow, and less fitted for social circumambulation. Over this are chambers for students.

G. Dyer *History of the University and College of Cambridge* 1814

QUEENS' COLLEGE President's Lodge

Queens' College was established when Queen Margaret petitioned King Henry VI with a request for its foundation. However, the college was completed by Queen Elizabeth, the consort of King Edward IV, hence the placing of the apostrophe in the name of the college.

QUEENS' COLLEGE Hall

Don't take seats which have been reserved, or attempt to sit at a boating or footer table for which you are unqualified.

Don't audibly criticise the menu or comment on its items, nor attempt to translate the remarks it contains. It will only appear that you are unaccustomed to dine out.

Don't joke with the waiters. They are apt to grow familiar if encouraged.

Don't forget that an occasional tip to the waiter will not be wasted.

The Fresher's Don't: to Freshers at Cambridge, these Remarks and Hints are Addressed in all Courtesy by a Sympathiser

The sundial table reads:

1	2	3	4	5	6	7	8	9	10	11	12	13	14	15
048	136	224	312	40	448	536	624	712	80	848	936	1024	1112	120
16	17	18	19	20	21	22	23	24	25	26	27	28	29	30

QUEENS' COLLEGE SUNDIAL *above*, OLD COURT *right*

…Queens' College is old but a stately and lofty building.

CELIA FIENNES *The Journeys of Celia Fiennes c.1697*

Old Court was completed in 1449 and is a fine example of medieval brickwork.
The dial, one of the finest sundials in the country, was added in 1733.

MILL POOL *above,* THE ANCHOR *right*

…the cool, quiet loitering that seems the style of boating to which
the mile of river threading the town and college precincts from Jesus
Lock to the Town Mill is dedicated. Boats for this are obtainable in
Silver Street and at Garrett Hostel Bridge.

JOSEPH CLARKE ISARD
The Illustrated Guide to Cambridge and Neighbourhood by a Resident of Trinity c.1889

RIVER CAM L<small>AUNDRESS</small> G<small>REEN</small> *left*, N<small>EWNHAM</small> R<small>OAD</small> *above*

As its name implies, this piece of common ground was used by the local washerwomen and college laundries for the drying of their washing. For this privilege a fee of one shilling a year was paid to the City Corporation and the laundry women had to erect their own posts and lines. The custom died out in Edwardian times but for many years the area continued to be used at spring-cleaning time for the beating of rugs and carpets.

SHEEP'S GREEN

…the most enchanting is the
exploration of the grassy, shady
windings above Crusoe's Island –
the first stretch of which above the
Town Bathing Shed has so won the
popular favour as to be dubbed
'Paradise'. The necessity of passing
the three bathing-sheds…is, of
course, a slight drawback if ladies be
of the party; but it is commonly
considered sufficiently disposed of
by a deft wielding of the parasol.

Joseph Clarke Isard
*The Illustrated Guide to Cambridge and
Neighbourhood by a Resident of Trinity*
*c.*1889

DARWIN COLLEGE
THE OLD GRANARY

…the architect insisted on …making the dining-room as far as possible from the kitchen, and the bathroom as far as possible from the hot-water boiler. This particular architect was quite explicit about it: he wrote a book on house design, in which he said: '*The coal store should be placed as far as possible from the kitchen, in order to induce economy in the use of fuel.*'

GWEN RAVERAT
Period Piece: a Cambridge Childhood
1952

The Old Granary was converted to a house by Charles Darwin's son George. It became part of Darwin College in the 1960s.

GRANTCHESTER

…would I were

In Grantchester, in Grantchester! –

Some, it may be, can get in touch

With Nature there, or earth, or such…

I only know that you may lie

Day long and watch the Cambridge sky,

And, flower-lulled in sleepy grass,

Hear the cool lapse of hours pass,

Until the centuries blend and blur…

…oh! yet

Stands the Church clock at ten-to-three?

And is there honey still for tea?

RUPERT BROOKE
From 'The Old Vicarage, Grantchester'
1912

TRUMPINGTON

At Trumpington, nat fer fro Cantebrigge,

Ther goth a brook and over that a brigge,

Up-on the whiche brook ther stant a melle;

And this is verray soth that I yow telle.

A Miller was ther dwelling many a day…

GEOFFREY CHAUCER
From The Reeves Tale
in *The Canterbury Tales*
1387

ANGLESEY ABBEY
LODE

The abbey was established as an Augustinian foundation in the thirteenth century. The buildings, or what was left of them after the Dissolution, passed to Thomas Hobson, the Cambridge Carrier and later to Sir George Downing, whose estates went to the founding of Downing College. The house is surrounded by wonderful gardens, with an arboretum, statues, and spectacular summer herbaceous borders.

GIRTON COLLEGE

She has 'put her gown on' at Girton,

She is learned in Latin and Greek,

But lawn tennis she plays with a skirt on

That the prudish remark with a shriek.

In her accents, perhaps, she is weak

(Ladies *are*, one observes with a sigh),

But in Algebra – there she's unique,

But her forte's to evaluate π.

ANDREW LANG
From 'Ballade of the Girton Girl'
1890

AMERICAN CEMETERY
MADINGLEY

Sleep peacefully

you friendly dead

held deep in Cambridge clay;

The years have covered you

in shrouds of Autumn gold

and anniversaries

paid for with your lives.

GEORGE KERRIDGE

Sidney Sussex College

Acknowledgements

Every effort has been made to secure permissions from copyright owners to use the extracts of text featured in this book.

Any subsequent correspondence should be sent to Jarrold Publishing at the following address: Jarrold Publishing, Whitefriars, Norwich NR3 1TR

page

13 From *Cambridgeshire, Huntingdonshire and the Isle of Ely* by E. A. R. Ennion. Published by Robert Hale, 1951.

30 (left) From *The Architecture of Southern England* by John Julius Norwich. Published by Macmillan, 1985. Reproduced by kind permission of the author.

39 (left) From *The Night Climbers of Cambridge* by Whipplesnaith. Published by Chatto & Windus, 1953.

45 (left) From *Cambridgeshire –*

A Shell Guide by Norman Scarfe. Published by Faber & Faber, 1983. Reproduced by kind permission of the author.

49 (top) From *The Cambridge, Ely and King's Lynn Road: The Great Fenland Highway* by Charles G. Harper. Published by Chapman & Hall, 1902.

50 (right) From *The Cantab* by Shane Leslie. Published by Chatto & Windus, 1926.

52 (right) From *The Architecture of Southern England* by John Julius Norwich. Published by Macmillan, 1985. Reproduced by kind permission of the author.

61 (right) From *The Architecture of Southern England* by John Julius Norwich. Published by Macmillan, 1985. Reproduced by kind permission of the author.

62 (right) From *The Cambridge, Ely and King's Lynn Road: The Great Fenland Highway*

by Charles G. Harper. Published by Chapman & Hall, 1902.

68 (right) Extract from the work *The Romance of the Cambridge College* by Francis Gribble. (First published 1913 by Mills & Boon Ltd). © 1913 Francis Gribble. Used with permission of Harlequin, Mills & Boon Ltd.

71 (right) Extract from the work *The Romance of the Cambridge College* by Francis Gribble. (First published 1913 by Mills & Boon Ltd). © 1913 Francis Gribble. Used with permission of Harlequin, Mills & Boon Ltd.

77 From *Cambridge Past and Present* by Brian W. Downs. Published by Methuen, 1926.

81 (left) From *The Architecture of Southern England* by John Julius Norwich. Published by Macmillan, 1985. Reproduced by kind permission of the author.

85 From *The Cambridge, Ely and King's*

Lynn Road: The Great Fenland Highway by Charles G. Harper. Published by Chapman & Hall, 1902.

87 (left) From *Down Your Street: Cambridge Past and Present* by Sara Payne. Published by Pevensey Press, 1983. Reproduced by permission of David & Charles Ltd.

92 (bottom) From *Cambridgeshire, Huntingdonshire and the Isle of Ely* by E. A. R. Ennion. Published by Robert Hale, 1951.

97 (right) From *Sacheverell Sitwell's England* by Sacheverell Sitwell. Published by Little Brown (Orbis), 1986. Reproduced by permission of David Higham Associates.

99 (left) From *The Cambridge Review*, 1934. Reproduced by permission of The Cambridge Review Committee.

113 From *Period Piece: a Cambridge Childhood* by Gwen Raverat. Published by Faber & Faber, 1952. Reproduced by kind permission of the copyright holders.

Bibliography

Editions and dates in this bibliography are those of the items that have been examined. In some cases earlier editions have significant differences to those listed here.

Arnold, Frederick: *Oxford and Cambridge and their Colleges.*
Religious Tract Society 1873.

Bickerdyke, John: *With the Best Intentions: a Tale of Undergraduate Life.*
W. Swan Sonnenschein and Co., 1884

Bristed, Charles Astor: *Five Years in an*

The Saxon tower of St Bene't's Church, the oldest building in Cambridgeshire

English University. First Published 1851; 3rd edition, Sampson Low, Marston Low & Searle, 1873.

Brooke, Rupert: 'The Old Vicarage, Grantchester' is in *Cambridge Poets 1900-1913, an Anthology,* chosen by Aelfrida Tillyard. W. Heffer & Sons Ltd, 1913.

Cambridge Official Guide. Revised reprint, Jarrold Publishing, 1997.

The Cambridge Review. 6 June 1934.

Chaucer, Geoffrey: *The Complete Works of Geoffrey Chaucer.* Oxford, Clarendon Press, 1900.

Coleridge, Samuel Taylor: 'Lines on an Autumnal Evening', is in *A Book of Cambridge Verse,* edited by E. E. Kellett, Cambridge University Press, 1911.

A Concise and Accurate Description of the University, Town, and County of Cambridge: Containing a Particular History of the Colleges and Public Buildings, Their Founders and Benefactors: A New and Improved edition. J. Archdeacon, 1785.

Conybeare, Edward: *Highways and Byways in Cambridge and Ely.* Macmillan and Co. Ltd, 1923.

Crutwell, Revd C.: *A Tour Through the Whole Island of Great Britain; Divided into Journeys* (6 Vols). G. and J. Robinson, 1801.

Darwin, Charles: *The Autobiography of Charles Darwin, 1809–1882, with Original Omissions Removed.* Edited with Appendix and Notes by his Granddaughter, Nora Barlow. Collins, 1958.

Defoe, Daniel: *A Tour Through the Whole Island of Great Britain, 1724-26.* J. M. Dent, 1928.

Downs, Brian W.: *Cambridge Past and Present.* Methuen, 1926.

Duncombe, J.: 'An Evening Contemplation in a College' is in *Socius: The Cambridge Tart: Epigramatic and Satiric-Poetical Effusions & Dainty Morsels Served up by Cantab on Various Occasions, Dedicated the Members of the University of Cambridge.* James Smith, 1823.

Dyer, G: *History of the University and College of Cambridge including Notices Relating to the Founders and Eminent Men.* Longman, Hurst, Rees, Orme and Brown, 1814.

The Eastern Counties Railway Illustrated Guide. James Truscott, 1851.

Ennion, E. A. R.: *Cambridgeshire, Huntingdonshire and the Isle of Ely.*

Trinity Street

Robert Hale, 1951.

Everett, William: *On the Cam: Lectures on the University of Cambridge in England.* Ward Lock and Tyler, 1869.

Fiennes, Celia: *The Illustrated Journeys of Celia Fiennes,* edited by Christopher Morris. Macdonald, 1982.

The Fresher's Don't: to Freshers at Cambridge, these Remarks and Hints are Addressed in all Courtesy by a Sympathiser. 13th edition. Redin & Co., [nd].

The Granta, 31 May 1889.

Gray, Thomas: Letters is in *In Praise of Cambridge: an Anthology for Friends,* compiled by Mervyn Horder.

Frederick Muller, 1952.

Gribble, Francis: *The Romance of the Cambridge College*. Mills & Boon, 1913.

Handbook for Essex, Suffolk, Norfolk and Cambridgeshire. 2nd edition, John Murray, 1875.

Harper, Charles G.: *The Cambridge, Ely and King's Lynn Road: The Great Fenland Highway*. Chapman & Hall, 1902.

Harraden, R. B.: *History and Description of the University of Cambridge*.

Free School Lane

R. B. Harraden, 1822.

Hints to the Fresh-men at the University of Cambridge. 3rd edition, 1807.

How to See Cambridge: a Really Useful and Interesting Guide to the Town and University. R. I. Severs, 1928.

Isard, Joseph Clarke: *The Illustrated Guide to Cambridge and Neighbourhood by a Resident of Trinity*. Jarrold & Sons, 1889.

James, Henry: *Portraits of Places*. Macmillan, 1883.

Kerridge, George: 'Sleep peacefully you friendly dead' is on display at the American Military Cemetery, Madingley. *The Lancet*: 28 April 1866

Lang, Andrew: *Poetical Works*, edited by Mrs Lang in four volumes. Longmans, Green and Co., 1923

Lawrence, Alfred Harry: *Reminiscences of Cambridge Life by D. C.* London, for private circulation only, 1889.

Leslie, Shane: *The Cantab*. Chatto & Windus, 1926.

Mee, Arthur: *The Kings England – Cambridgeshire*. Hodder & Stoughton, 1937.

Milton, John: 'An Apology for Smectymnuus, 1641' is in *Five Tracts Relating to Church Government, published*

in the year 1641. Amsterdam, 1694

A New Pictorial and Descriptive Guide to Cambridge and District. Ward Lock, 1928.

Norwich, John Julius: *The Architecture of Southern England*. Macmillan, 1985.

Payne, Sara: *Down Your Street: Cambridge Past and Present. Vol. 1 Central Cambridge*. Pevensey Press, 1983.

Pepys, Samuel: *Diary and Correspondence of Samuel Pepys, F. R. S. Secretary to the Admiralty in the Reign of Charles II and James II. With a Life and Notes by Richard, Lord Braybrooke* (4 Volumes). George Allen & Unwin Ltd, 1848–49, reprinted 1929.

Raverat, Gwen: *Period Piece: a Cambridge Childhood*. Faber & Faber, 1952.

Reeve, F. A.: *Cambridge from the River*. Newton & Denny, 1977.

Salmon, Thomas: *The Foreigners Companion Through the Universities of Cambridge and Oxford*. William Owen, 1748.

Scarfe, Norman: *Cambridgeshire – A Shell Guide*. Faber & Faber, 1983.

Sitwell, Sacheverell: *Sacheverell Sitwell's England*, edited by Michael Raeburn. Little, Brown & Co. (Orbis), 1986.

Smith, John: *Sketches of Cantabs*.

George Earle, 1849.

Stephen, Leslie: *Life of Henry Fawcett*. Smith Elder, 1885, and *Sketches from Cambridge, by a Don*. Macmillan, 1865.

Tennyson, Alfred: *Poetical Works, Including the Plays*. Oxford University Press, 1953.

Whipplesnaith (pseud): *The Night Climbers of Cambridge*. Chatto & Windus, 1953.

Wordsworth, William: *The Prelude: or Growth of a Poet's Mind*, edited by Ernest de Selincourt. 2nd edition, Oxford, Clarendon Press, 1959.

Beehives in the Fellows' Garden, Christ's College

Mathematical Bridge, Queens' College

Index

GROUNDCOVER
SERIES